Failing Forward in Student Affairs

Using Missteps to Guide Next Steps

FAILING FORWARD in STUDENT AFFAIRS
using missteps to guide next steps

LISA ENDERSBY
· SERIES EDITOR ·

TOM KRIEGLSTEIN, SABINA DeMATTEO
MELISSA RUIZ & JESSI FERGUSON
· BOOK EDITORS ·

SUE CAULFIELD
·ILLUSTRATOR·

Failing Forward in Student Affairs
Using Missteps to Guide Next Steps

Collaboratively Created By
Lisa Endersby – Series Editor
Sue Caulfield – Illustrator
Jessi Ferguson – Book Editor
Sabina De Matteo – Book Editor
Melissa Ruiz, MSW - Book Editor
Tom Krieglstein – Book Editor

Other Student Affairs Collective Books

Tracking is Trending: A Survival Guide to Assessment in Student Affairs

Trust the Journey - When and How to Move for Your Student Affairs Career

Beyond Meetings – Lessons and Success in Advising Student Organizations

Men in Student Affairs - Stories from 13 Student Affairs Professionals

From the Beginning: Perspectives from New and Emerging SA Pros

Hello My Name Is Committed: Stories About Dealing with Mental Illness in Student Affairs

All titles can be viewed and ordered at
www.StudentAffairsCollective.org/Bookstore

A Student Affairs Collective Book

Failing Forward in Student Affairs: Using Missteps to Guide Next Steps

Printed in the United States of America

Design by Student Affairs Collective

10 9 8 7 6 5 4 3

Student Affairs Collective
www.StudentAffairsCollective.org
info@studentaffairscollective.org
Phone: (877) 479-4385
Fax: (206) 337-0259

>> **Contact for bulk order discounts** <<

About The Student Affairs Collective

As with all great ideas, the Student Affairs Collective (www.StudentAffairsCollective.org) began as a series of doodles on the back of a napkin by Tom Krieglstein and Kevin Prentiss in 2005. The vision was, and still is, to create the ultimate online community of student affairs professionals in which everyone is both a teacher and student at the same time, helping each other play, learn and grow together to collectively reach higher levels of success.

In the beginning, Tom and Kevin wrote all the content. They then bribed their student affairs friends with cookies and digital unicorns to help them write more content, and slowly, over time, an engaged community developed. The SA Collective started to become the go-to place online for student affairs professionals to receive and share knowledge from their peers. The growth remained steady, and then Twitter came along...

In 2009, over lunch with Debra Sanborn at an Iowa coffee shop, Tom pitched the idea of a weekly chat via Twitter for student affairs professionals. Debra nodded excitedly at the idea (as she does with all new ideas), and a couple weeks later, on Oct 8th, 2009, the first #SAChat happened with 15 people and 50 tweets.

Since then, the SAC, which is what the cool kids call it, has grown to a community of thousands of student affairs professionals, stretching international borders and all functional areas of the field. We now have a podcast, a book club, a jobs board, a member directory with learning communities, a weekly newsletter, Tweetups, and the #SAChat Awards. Through it all, the SAC continues to focus on creating the best online, low cost, peer-to-peer learning network for student affairs professionals.

Now, it's your turn to jump in and be a part of the family and help us create the next ten years of awesomeness. As a bonus, you'll laugh, smile, create friendships, and grow a positive national reputation for yourself and your work. Then, when you go on to change the world, we'll get to say you first shared your potential with us by helping fellow student affairs professionals be even more amazing!

Tom Krieglstein
Founder, Student Affairs Collective
@TomKrieglstein

How To Use This Book

While this entire book is focused around one main theme, each individual author takes on a unique perspective around this theme. Some chapters might be totally relevant to your current situation and others not so much. Reading this book from beginning to end is probably not going to be as valuable as looking at the table of contents and skipping ahead to the chapters that are most relevant to your current situation.

Share The Love Online

We love knowing when fellow student affairs professionals are taking their professional development into their own hands. If you take a photo of yourself with this book and share it online via one of the channels listed below, we'll send you digital unicorns in return!

On Twitter, post your photo and:
>   Use the #SAChat hashtag
>   Tag the @The_SA_Blog account

On Facebook, post your photo to these groups:
Student Affairs Professionals >
https://www.facebook.com/groups/2204795643/
Student Affairs Collective >
https://www.facebook.com/SACollective

Acknowledgements

To our storytellers

Thank you for saying yes. Thank you for your courage. Thank you for telling stories that we don't often share. Your vulnerability is inspiring.

A special thank you to Tom, Sabina, and the Student Affairs Collective team for creating space for these stories and for all your hard work in putting this book together. I hope this book inspires persistence and patience as you travel your path. Together, let's learn that failure will propel us further, not hold us back. Together, let's Fail Forward.

- Lisa Endersby

table of contents

introduction.

Introduction - Lisa Endersby

"Success is not final. Failure is not fatal. It is the courage to continue that counts." (Winston Churchill)

I wanted to write about failure because everyone else was, but I didn't want to write like anyone else. There was so much more that needed to be said. I didn't want to examine failure as an action or an event. I wanted to talk about failure as an emotion, an identity, and a place we seem to find ourselves returning to, over and over again.

The idea for #SAFailsForward grew out of conversations with colleagues and friends. I was drawn to the idea of failure after working to shake it off as an identifier; as a characteristic I would use to describe myself in the same way I would rhyme off my age, eye colour, and date of birth. I knew that others were also carrying mistakes and missteps as permanent measures of their ability and self worth, defining themselves by an event or two that interrupted a much more positive and optimistic narrative. Too often, we depersonalize mistakes yet internalize failure - there is something in that subtle shift in vocabulary that can turn a teachable moment into an impassable chasm. The more

11

personal and internal the failure became, the more hidden and tucked away it remained. The very darkness that we used to shield ourselves from the discomfort of failure allowed it to grow and fester.

My hope for this book is to have failure step out of the shadows and for our stories to be completely in the spotlight. There is no place to hide in Brene Brown's arena, and as harsh and unforgiving as this spotlight is, these pieces are deeply, painfully, and wonderfully human. They show flaws, they celebrate effort over perfection, and they model a depth of courage that I have been humbled to inspire and encourage. This book is about bringing light to failure and keeping it there - boldly and unapologetically sharing, examining, and reflecting on our failures. There are no platitudes here. Each author has told their truth, the good, bad, ugly, and everything in between.

I hope, as you read these stories, that you consider them as guideposts rather than points of comparison. Just as success is personal, so is failure (perhaps even more so). There is no pride in failing less (or more). There are no rewards for learning more, or more quickly, after each mistake. Consider each story for the author's courage, their self compassion, and their willingness to learn, try, fail, succeed, learn, and try again. I am so honoured to have played a role in bringing these stories to you and into the world. They are meant to be told, and need to be heard. Failure can only set us back if we let it. Together, I invite you to join us in failing forward.

 A voracious reader from a young age, I (attempt to) balance living in my own head with externally processing anything and everything with anyone and everyone. Taking on the title of 'Advocate for Awesome', my work in higher education spans defining and chasing student success in leadership development, career services, community engagement and, my most recent love, assessment. Follow her on twitter @lmendersby

Re-creating Narratives of Failure - Summer King Mattina

Your tornado may cause you fear
my tornado
is cause for dreaming more
my tornado
is not your tornado
is not your tornado

- from Tornado, a poem by Gene Pfeiffer

This book has features very personal stories of personal and professional failure. Many of these stories have portable and immediate lessons to instruct us, or words of wisdom to inspire us as we march through time. I am humbled by each of our contributors; you rock.

My story does not fit into this category, though. There is no great redemption, no moral or professional high ground. There is no victory. **There is, in the end, just a life—my life.** I want to tell some stories about my life, and of my failure, even though I know it does not fit neatly into the theme of this book and might not immediately resonate with you, my audience. I want to use my story to illustrate the potentially harmful effects of isolating perceived failure from its larger context, and **I want to challenge us to remember that failure, like any values-based construct, is intersectional—it is social, cultural, and deeply personal.** I want us to examine more critically the ways we define failure and utilize those definitions in our conversations with colleagues and students. I want us to recognize the privilege that comes with re-framing stories and directing those narratives. Like many of you, **I believe in the liberating power of transparency; I also know the silencing power of unrecognized bias and microaggressions.** We can, in sharing our stories of failure and failing forward, inadvertently silence others who may contently embody the very definition of failure we believe we overcame. I want to encourage us to practice mindful, tender storytelling, most especially in our work with students. **Let none of us feel as though we must hide in plain sight.**

"Let none of us feel as though we must hide in plain sight."

To understand why I feel this way and why I think all of this merits examination in the first place, it might help to know a bit about me. By some folks' standards for failure, I am, today, a consummate loser: I'm nearing 40, but I have not started my PhD nor have I ascended beyond the "entry level." I'm on my second marriage, and, as of this writing, I could stand to lose about 20 pounds. I don't dress for the job I want; I dress for the budget I have. I possess modest financial means. I drive a car that needs a bit of body work. I have been told that my hair is too long and my skirts are too short and my laugh is too loud and I don't "act my age." I haven't attended a national conference in years, but I have been to a quite a few concerts.

Despite the external standards that would have me do more and be more and alwaysalwaysalways pushpushpush growgrowgrow nownownow, I am content with every fluctuating and static aspect of my life. **This, some might say, is my most staggering failure of all—that I am able to find satisfaction amidst so many personal and professional shortcomings.**

Now, to understand how and why all of this has come to be, it may help to know a bit more about me. Perhaps I can even redeem myself a bit. I have been working in student affairs for a short time; I share the "new professional" descriptor with people 15 years my junior. Before I completed my master's degree in 2012, I spent ten years working on my bachelor's degree as a part-time, employed, non-traditional, first-generation, commuter student. Despite having been accepted into a prestigious university my senior year of high school, I started my post-secondary education at a middling community college. I can hear the readers' wheels turning...knowing this about me creates a framework for understanding, a series of reliable statistical probabilities developed from research on lived realities.

But to really understand how and why THAT came to be, it helps to understand MY lived reality. Twenty years ago, I became one of the worst kinds of social pariahs: I became an unmarried pregnant teenage female, a poster child for failure. **I had failed my parents, my public education, my community, my abstinence-based sex ed program, my friends.** I was instructed to believe that I had failed myself. Words like "white trash," "slut," "failure," "ruined," "disappointment" were flung at and about me by those closest to me. **When I strode across the stage at my high school graduation, my pregnant belly and honors cords commemorating my stunted potential, I felt overwhelming shame.**

And, to understand how and why THAT came to be, it helps to understand the myriad of ways abuse, and poverty, and generational familial dysfunction conditions children. **Statistically, I was predestined to fail.** My parents had not failed forward from their own life experiences, and did not encourage their children to fail forward. Life was hard. I received food stamps and free school lunches and still managed to know hunger. I had tremendous teachers and friends and still managed to know the isolation of hiding in plain sight. **I was sad a lot.**

Working through that morass has created in me a sensitivity to how others define failure, and an awareness of how I do and do not meet or exceed those marks in any given moment. I am often confronted with students who share with me stories of their young friends, cousins, and neighbors getting pregnant and "ruining" their lives; I must explain myself. I am confronted by colleagues who mistake me for a traditionally-educated practitioner with a traditional SA trajectory; I must explain myself. I am confronted by people who assume that the photos on my desk are not of my son, but of a brother or boyfriend, and again I must explain myself. **I am confronted by people who assume that my desire to promote equitable post-secondary access and opportunity exists because I am a liberal and white-privileged "do-gooder," not because I want to pay the benefits of my own struggle forward.** Over and over and again and again I explain myself. Those assumptions about me often feel like expectations. **Not living up or down to those expectations can feel like failure in and of itself.**

It is hard work, grappling with other people's definitions of success and failure while simultaneously trying to establish your own. Attempting to live an authentic life further complicates this process. I don't see my life as having come to some triumphant "forward" moment where I conquered my upbringing or broke free from my statistically-ordained destiny. Underneath all of the talk of failure and success, there is just me, living my life as well and authentically as I can live it. **And that, for me, is enough, even if it looks like failure or inertia to you.** Forward is a construct. Failure can be a lie. My tornado is not your tornado, is not your tornado.

 Summer King Mattina happily serves as an Academic Advisor for Parks College of Engineering, Aviation, and Technology at Saint Louis University. She enjoys rock and roll, rocky beaches, and rocking chairs. She also likes stone soup. Get to know her by connecting on Twitter @SummerMattina.

FEEDBACK is a GIFT 🎁

Feedback is a Gift - Julie Payne-Kirchmeier

There are moments when you mess up in your career, and you realize it right away. You know what I mean – you accidentally hit "reply all" on a snarky response (not good), you say something you **think** is funny (and it's not), or you print a publication with a massive typo in the first line. These are the things you notice – things you can point to – and the things you can fix either with an apology, by shrugging it off, or by re-printing 200 copies of a handout (you know you've done it).

Then there are the things it takes you years to realize, and only after many cycles and episodes does it finally hit you – like a bolt of lightning. **These are the "Fail Forward" moments, the ones that change you forever.**

I've always been a hard worker. As a young professional, I was hard-wired to run 100 miles an hour straight ahead, making massive lists and setting goals like mad. More often than not, I would accomplish these goals, and then start setting more. I loved the feeling of accomplishment – and quite frankly, I'm really good at it.

What I am not good at – AT ALL – is stopping and reflecting on how experiences or moments have impacted me as a person or a professional. Logically, I know reflection is critical for development – but it requires something that I was never comfortable with: feedback. **I hated feedback, and after years of hitting the wall, I finally figured out why.**

I was obsessed with perfection. My lists had to be completely checked off. Every detail had to be perfect. I used every kind of planning system imaginable to accomplish tasks more quickly and efficiently. Any error was overly-scrutinized, and I'd beat myself up about it for weeks. While mistakes never stopped me from trying again, I would work SO FREAKING HARD to make things perfect, that I would exhaust myself. My second year out of graduate school, I was working 14 hour days. At my next job, I "improved" and got that down to 12 hour days.

"I hated feedback, and after years of hitting the wall, I finally figured out why."

In order to protect myself from negativity, and to maintain my perceived levels of productivity and good work, I would actively avoid feedback. I was so afraid to hear the things that were wrong with a program, event or project, that I would over-plan every detail, or be overly-critical of any tiny thing that went wrong. My self-evaluations were unusually harsh, and any assessment results I received about a program I would make sure to grab first so that I could beat myself up about it behind the scenes. I would front load my conversations with my supervisors with all of the bad things about a program in order to avoid hearing negative feedback from them. **I never saw these moments as development opportunities;** I saw them as moments where I had to be on the offensive, or I would get fired.

What I didn't understand was that I was working hard to avoid taking a hard look at myself. When I finally accepted that feedback wasn't the enemy, but rather a gift given to you by people who care, I was finally able to listen. After talking to my trusted friends and colleagues, and actually hearing what they said, I finally realized **I was so obsessed with perfection, I forgot to be good.** I thought that if anyone saw a tiny mistake before I did, or provided me with constructive feedback about my own performance before I was able to recognize it in myself, I had failed. **I had constricted myself to a world where I could only win or lose.**

As I've grown in my life and career, I've adopted the philosophy that feedback is a good thing, that it truly is a gift others give to you, and that these insights into who I am, how I'm performing and what I can change are so incredibly beneficial. The people who give me feedback are mirrors – causing me to reflect in genuine and intentional ways – and helping me change for the better.

Recently, my friend, mentor and colleague, Dr. Kathy Collins, posted the following: "I never lose…..either I win, or I learn."

The truth is, **those who actively seek out feedback with true curiosity and openness are the people who win, because these are the people who learn.** Again – I'm not great at it yet – but at least this time around I'm not alone in the journey. I have my mirrors to help guide me along the way. And that is the greatest gift of all.

Julie Payne-Kirchmeier has been the Assistant Vice President for Auxiliary Services at Northwestern University since January 2012. She oversees residential services, dining, Norris, Student Affairs Information Technology and Saferide. Before coming to Northwestern, Payne-Kirchmeier served as the Director of University Housing and Assistant Provost for the University College at Southern Illinois University Carbondale. Find her on twitter @jpkirchmeier

failing by omission

Failing by Omission - Mallory Bower

The failures that haunt me are the ones that no one knows about. They're the times I failed to ask for help, to speak up, or to take a risk.

I call this **failing by omission.**

Recognizing this brand of failure can be tricky, because you haven't exactly fallen flat on your face. It usually begins with a bit of insecurity and a nagging case of the "what ifs." Sometimes the losses are so small that they go undetected for a long while. But trust me, they add up.

- I missed out on job opportunities because I didn't apply.
- I settled for lower salaries because I didn't negotiate or ask for a raise.
- I let someone else take credit for my work and I didn't speak up.
- I lost my love for a job because I didn't ask for help when I was burned out.
- I missed out on making new connections because I was too intimidated to introduce myself.

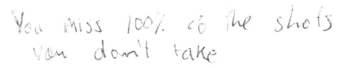

You miss 100% of the shots you don't take

- ☐ I hurt dear friends because of the words I didn't say.
- ☐ I lose the lottery every dang time... because I don't play.

What if I applied, asked, introduced, reached out, took a gamble? I'll never really know. But the important piece to any type of failure is that we learn something from it. If we're lucky, we learn not to dwell on the past, but instead, to channel our hopes through those "what-ifs."

"I call this **failing by omission.**"

What if we avoid getting stuck by taking a single step? What if we embrace discomfort instead of being paralyzed by fear? What if we think, "What's the worst that could happen?" What if we give it all we've got instead of wondering what could have been?

What if we don't fail, but succeed in ways we've never imagined?

 Mallory is a university career coach and friendraiser who's on a mission to find out what makes people "tick." Connect with her on Twitter (@MalloryBower) and via her blog (mallorybower.com).

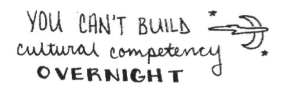

You Can't Build Cultural Competency Overnight - Jessika Chi

We need to reframe our concept of failure. It's OK to fail. Truly. It's through failing that we learn, grow, and develop. Yet, the fear of failure continues to hold people back. **One area in which I see this consistently is the lack of engagement with diversity and cultural competency education – because people fear that they have or will "fail" in these conversations.**

Working in multicultural affairs, I see time and time again a hesitancy to engage in the dialogue because people are too afraid of doing and/or saying the "wrong" things. I often hear "I don't know what to say" or "I don't want to make a mistake."**It's OK to make mistakes!** It's OK to "fail." It's actually part of the process. **We all make mistakes – we all sometimes do and say the wrong things, even diversity and social justice educators.** We are in the profession of education because at our core, we are lifelong learners and we value learning. So, we shouldn't hide, duck, ignore, or brush off these opportunities to learn. **We need to take RISKS and ENGAGE in the conversation because to not engage in diversity and cultural competency education is not an option.** If we are afraid to fail, we will keep failing forever.

For those who are afraid to fail in this area:

We probably have shared or similar experiences.

1. Have confidence in your ability to engage in cultural conversations.

Identity and culture play a critical role in the work that we do with students. We all have intersecting identities – so let's talk about them! Speak from your experience and tell your truths and be willing to listen, understand, and learn from the experiences of others. What's there to be afraid of? **You can't fail at BEING YOU.**

2. It's a process – give yourself, and others, grace.

I meant it when I said that failure is part of the process, and the process is all that matters. There aren't any "right" outcomes or answers. So know that we are all learning together and committed to supporting each other through this journey.

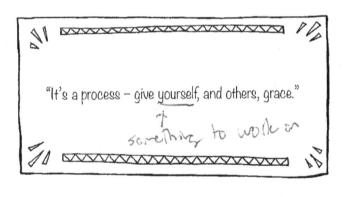

"It's a process – give yourself, and others, grace."
something to work on

3. Cultural competency doesn't just build overnight.

You don't get competent by just attending one training, so continue to engage in ongoing opportunities. Your competency, confidence, and capacity will continue to build up over time.

And a couple thoughts for my fellow diversity and social justice educators that encounter this issue:

1. Share why.

Part of the reason why people are afraid to say or do the "wrong" thing is because **some people approach this work by policing others and letting them know what they just said or did was offensive without explaining why.** If you approach this work from an elitist or expert model, it will shut people down and make them not want to even engage in the conversation. **This work is not about policing people's actions or words; instead, it's about getting people to understand the issues and how they can be a part of the change.**

2. Invite everyone to the conversation.

Sometimes we don't know who our allies will be or sometimes we've already made up our minds on who is or isn't an ally. Don't assume and pre-judge people – risk asking. **You never know.** Your invite can go a long way in making those who might hesitate out of fear of failing feel included and valued in the conversation.

3. Engage with *all* students about issues of diversity.

As Gwen Dungy said at the NASPA Multicultural Institute, "we are failing our students, all of our students, if we are just letting students of Color hide out in multicultural affairs offices." Lee Mun Wah also emphasizes that we are failing our White students when we only focus our efforts on our students of Color without educating all students about issues of diversity and social justice. **Everyone should have the opportunity to build their cultural competency.**

4. Continue to share with others moments where you have "failed."

Part of the beauty of failing forward is to show that we all at some point have "failed" and it's how we bounce back and learn from that experience that matters. This is especially true in diversity education work. It puts people at ease if you are willing to be vulnerable and share moments where you've said or done the wrong things and how you responded to those situations.

People might say it's uncomfortable to talk about issues like racism, sexism, heterosexism, etc. on campus. Well, I say it's more uncomfortable to live with it and have it go unaddressed. We must keep moving forward in the areas of social justice. We must keep **failing forward** – don't let the fear of failure paralyze us. Who's in?

 Jessika Chi is the Program Manager for the Department of Inclusion and Multicultural Engagement at Lewis & Clark College in Portland, OR. She is deeply committed to life-long learning and advocating for social and educational equity. She is dedicated to empowering others to create lives of meaning and purpose. Connect with her on twitter: @jessikachi!

THE DRAWING BOARD
changed

The Drawing Board Changed - Juhi Bhatt

When I entered into my undergraduate career in 2005, I was told that a degree in education would never fail me as teaching was not a dying field. Teachers would always be needed. Fast forward four years to my graduation from The College of NJ, wherein I graduated Cum Laude, in the top 15% of my class, Dean's list for all eight semesters and was inducted into three honor societies. **Suffice to say I did not think I would have a hard time finding a teaching position, but I had spoken too soon.** In 2009, when I graduated with a Bachelor of Music degree, the teaching field had sunk to an all-time low. Furthermore, as a music educator I had even fewer positions to apply for as most schools usually only had one to two music educators.

That summer, I applied for what must have been about 80 music teaching positions and I kid you not, I received two calls for interviews. **It's hard to not think of yourself as a failure when the education you worked so hard to achieve, at such a high academic level, does not seem to be benefiting you at all.** I began to question the amount of time I had spent on my education at TCNJ. I saw my fellow classmates obtaining jobs and wondered what I had one wrong. **I felt like I had let my parents**

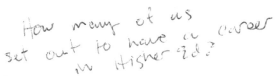

How many of us set out to have a career in Higher Ed.?

down as they had supported my education and here I was unable to find a position in the field.

In the end the only position I was offered was a part time, one day a week K-6 general music teaching position at a local school district close to home. So there I was, a 22 year old young professional, teaching only one day a week. In those first few months, since I had so much spare time, I began to think about going back for my masters sooner than I had originally intended.

So how did I fall into student affairs? By chance. **I ended up going to Montclair State for my Masters in Counseling, Student Affairs/Counseling in Higher Education, because others had told me I was a "good listener".** My fieldwork for the program brought me to Bergen Community College. I started off as a career counselor who by luck ended up assisting the now Dean of Judicial Affairs and Student Life.

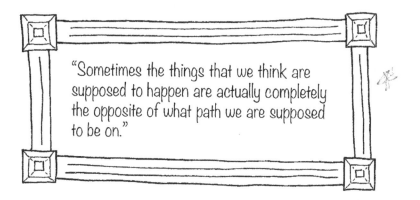

"Sometimes the things that we think are supposed to happen are actually completely the opposite of what path we are supposed to be on."

That's when and where I fell in love with student conduct, and honestly, student life. I never knew such offices even existed on campus. I thought that graduation was just a thing that happened but now as I meet with students who may be suspended or assist in graduation ceremonies, I see the work that goes into such offices. The experience is overwhelming at times. But I always think back to the fact that had I gotten that full time teaching job, I would not be where I am today. **Sometimes the things that we think are supposed to happen are actually the complete opposite of the path we are supposed to be on.** Situations of failure bring about opportunities for change. When I believed I had failed at teaching because I could not get a full time teaching career, I went right back to the drawing board and suddenly the drawing board changed. These days, although I love working with children, I do not know how I would go back to teaching K-12.

Juhi Bhatt is currently the Coordinator of Student Conduct & Student Information at Bergen Community College. Along with being the conduct officer at the institution Juhi serves as the case manager for the Behavioral Intervention Team (BIT), supervisor of the student information desk with 10+ student workers, and as co-advisor to the Student Government Association (SGA). Within the Office of Student Life & Student Conduct Juhi assists with the planning and implementation of new student orientation and commencement. Juhi has been at BCC since spring 2011. She has her Bachelors in music education from The College of New Jersey, her Master's in counseling from Montclair State University and is currently pursuing her Doctorate of Education in higher education administration at Saint Peter's University. Follow Juhi on twitter @jbhatt12

moving foward
by looking back

Moving Forward by Looking Back - Dustin Ramsdell

Something I think about a lot is the past. **I was a history major as an undergraduate student, so I appreciate the story that each person has and the fact that everything that happens around us has a background story.** A professor shared a fun anecdote that explains this: He described the discipline of history as a "turtle on a fencepost", as to say that turtle could not have gotten up there on its own, so there is some story there we can explore. **Whether it is something that happened yesterday or two hundred years ago, there is a background story from which we learn and grow.**

Another great quote is **"Those who cannot remember the past are condemned to repeat it."** It applies to the history of us as a human race, but also our own personal stories. To simply forget whatever came before deprives us of an amazing learning experience. Granted, one has to be comfortable enough to take a hard look at themselves, but I think the results are very powerful. **Being able to analyze and scrutinize our own behavior and choices, especially with the help of a trusted confidant, is really one of the only ways to constantly grow and develop into the most prudent and self-aware person we can be.**

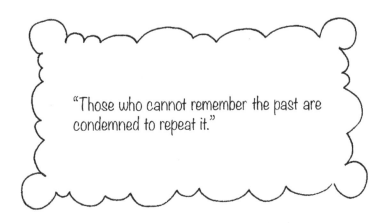

"Those who cannot remember the past are condemned to repeat it."

To give a personal example of how I've progressed and failed forward through self-reflection, last year, during my graduate program, I decided to put myself out there and jockeyed for multiple volunteer opportunities in the field. I wanted to be president of our graduate student organization for our student affairs program, an ACPA (American College personnel Association) ambassador and/or a TPE (The Placement Exchange) ambassador. **To make a long story short, I did not gain any of these positions.** On top of all this, I also struggled to find a NODA (National Orientation Directors Association) internship for the summer. I was pretty bummed out. It made me feel stupid for even trying and as if I was somehow less than my peers. My ego was checked and I was humbled even more than I usually was. I felt as though I didn't deserve anything because I wasn't good enough. **Looking back on it now, I know I needed to be humbled a bit. But, I was still able to have some awesome experiences, despite my perceived failure.** I worked at Rutgers for the summer, had a lot of fun and met amazing people (namely my partner) and realized the only reason I wanted some of those aforementioned opportunities in the first place was to just say I had them.

So, in order to be the best professionals and best people we can be, I think we all need to stop every once in awhile and take a look back at where we've been in order to better get where we're going, especially if that means coming to terms with our "failures". **Success is what we make of it and so is failure.** Success can be falling down and picking ourselves back up, enduring a storm, or just keeping positive even when we've been overlooked. **Failure can be staying safe, resting on your laurels, and keeping quiet.** I never give up, no matter what obstacles come my way. I'm impressed with myself in this regard; the courage to keep going comes up from somewhere deep inside me. When I look back, I didn't get what I thought I wanted, but in the end, through broadening my view of what failure means to me, I was able to grow from the experience. I encourage everyone out there to do the same and use those experiences to mentor our students. **By starting with ourselves and redefining our definitions of failure, we can provide some powerful life lessons for our students, which is what this is all about when it comes down to it.**

 Dustin is a recent graduate of the Rutgers University College Student Affairs Ed.M Program. He also is an alumni of University of Delaware, and currently works at Husson University in Maine. He is a proud nerd and self-affirmed "Higher Ed Geek" who is excited to connect with folks who share his love of deep conversations! Find out more at: about.me/dustin_ramsdell & follow him on Twitter, @HigherEd_Geek!

FAILURE AS A MENTOR

Failure as a Mentor - Sean Eddington

We live in a perception-driven society that dictates that we are only as good as what we produce. Outcomes rule the world around us, and need to be tidy, perfected, and fit into nice, little boxes. **Perfection and success are praised over struggle.** This stress to be perfect, to succeed (in other words, TO NOT FAIL) has created major issues in the world we live in. We are taught and socialized to avoid failure at all cost. Our favorite vulnerability guru, Brene Brown, writes, "Perfectionism is a self destructive and addictive belief system that fuels this primary thought: If I look perfect, and do everything perfectly, I can avoid or minimize the painful feelings of shame, judgment, and blame."

Failure has become synonymous with shame, and we must never been seen as weak. To be seen as weak is to be less than. To be worthless. We see this at play on our college campuses with skyrocketing mental health issues. Our students are literally harming themselves to get "A"s in their courses because anything less is a failure. This stress not only affects our students—it affects us!

We asked individuals within the #SAchat family to share their stories and struggles regarding mental health and wellbeing for #SAcommits. These stories and experiences are connected—they are stories all about grit. They represent individuals embracing and celebrating their collective struggles, gleaning lessons from each struggle, and using them as opportunities to **keep moving forward**. When we talk about embracing failure and struggles, we essentially are talking about failing forward. We need struggle to appreciate the successes. After all, as writer, Sandra Kring writes, "The tiny seed knew that in order to grow, it needed to be dropped in dirt, covered in darkness, and struggle to reach the light."

"When we talk about vulnerability, one way to be vulnerable is to share our stories of utter failure."

So, how do we fail? Sometimes it's in relationships. Maybe it's the sarcastic comment that came out a little too biting. It could be not meeting (or living up to) expectations. Or maybe it's failing to meet the training and mentoring needs of new professionals (**Hint:** Hold onto this thought because I will come back to it). The fact of the matter is that we all fail, make mistakes, and endure missteps daily. Each of us has struggles, and will fail. Some, like myself, will fail regularly. What is important is being able to rise and honor the failure. We must acknowledge failures when they come. They will hurt, but the pain will pass. Embracing failure and learning to respect and honor it and its lessons is a process. It takes a lot of courage to be willing to acknowledge your failures and shortcomings. **When we talk about vulnerability, one way to be vulnerable is to share our stories of utter failure.**

And boy, do I have stories!

My first few years as a professional were some of the best in my career thus far–not because I was wildly successful–but because I failed...A LOT. *(Real talk: I hated it while I was living through it, but, after time to process, I've become incredibly grateful for the experiences because it has made me a better professional and leader.)* I will always own the fact that I was a CHUMP during my first few years in the professional world. My second year was exceptionally difficult, as we had experienced heavy turnover. The senior leaders of our team had left, which meant that our team was relatively a rookie team. Being the whippersnapper that I am, I stepped into the leadership role, and started guiding and **trying** to mentor three new staff members. While my learning of the hall director-like position had been relatively easy, I had assumed it would be the same for our three new staff members. Spoiler alert: It was not the same. Processes, administrative tasks, and even student development practices were being questioned and sometimes "botched". I understood why we were performing certain tasks, but I could not find a way to explain it to the newer team members. Furthermore, I could not understand why the team that I was a de facto leader of was not performing efficiently. **Little things related to student services became arguments, and as I became**

more frustrated, my leadership dwindled and the team started to slowly implode.

It took a series of back and forth nasty e-mails before our boss intervened. My boss created a safe space for us to be vulnerable with one another. We all needed to air grievances, frustrations, and reset (both team climate and relationships). As a leader of this team, I felt like an absolute failure. I was unable to see that, like the students we work with, these new professionals would also have a developmental learning curve.

It was foolish and naive of me to believe that they would have the same learning experiences as me. I had not taken their experiences into account, and mentored them as though I was mentoring myself. In a sense, I neglected their stories and experiences. It was in these collective experiences during my second year that I began to learn some pretty awesome lessons that stick with me today:

1. When we train our professionals, it is important to remember that everyone's learning curve will be different.

> One-size-fits-all approaches to training do not work and can create issues. We also need to be able to clearly explain our WHY with our practices. Sometimes they'll be evident, and other times they'll need explanation.

2. It is important to know the stories of your team members.

> They matter, and can help guide training and practices. Everyone brings experiences to their teams, and if I had been more aware of this during my second year, it would not have been such a hard year for me professionally. Conversely, it also may not have been such a professionally developmental and formative year for me had we not had the struggle.

Henry Ford once stated, **"Failure is the opportunity to begin again, only this time, more wisely."** After our team hit the "Reset Button," we were able to become much more effective and efficient. Out students were able to see a shift in our team, and, as a reflection of my team's higher wellbeing, the students were happier and more academically successful. **Why? Because we failed in a big way.** It was hard and challenging, but it was an opportunity to rebuild the team. Early on in my career, a boss told me, "Every experience is a good experience—even if it is a bad experience—because you can learn from them." Had I not failed (and my team failed), I would not have had those experiences and learned those lessons so clearly. **Failure is, was, and will continue to be one of my best mentors.** Failure is good for you, and while it is painful, challenging, and [insert whatever word you deem adequate], failure is our greatest teacher. It can be our best source of inspiration, innovation, courage, and human connection. Through failure, we are able to learn, take risks, and keep moving forward. Look no further than Meet the Robinson's for an example in utilizing failure as a wonderful teacher. Just think, wouldn't it be neat to have a celebration for every time you failed?

Sean Eddington is an Academic Advisor for Exploratory Studies at Purdue University. In his work, Sean advises and mentors students to find their academic and career paths by offering them opportunities to explore the world around them. The core of his work with students is centered around the importance failing forward, resiliency, and wellbeing. Connect with him on Twitter @seanmeddington or on his blog: www.seaneddington.wordpress.com.

My Favorite Program Failure - Jade Perry

My boss took me to lunch on the first day of my graduate assistantship at Penn State Career Services and said, "We've completely ended the diversity program we've been running for about ten years. It wasn't working out. Our recruiters weren't getting the point of it, although they did enjoy it. **So, it's going to be up to you to create and implement our new diversity program. Welcome to the team!"**
I almost choked on my appetizer.

I knew that the older program, a speed networking session for students with diverse backgrounds, was one that my institution loved. I knew I'd get a lot of questions about why the program was ending. **Yet, this was a task I was happy to take on, although I was completely unsure of what would happen.**

Take one:

I looked at the structure of Penn State University and I thought about how it was decentralized, in certain respects. Each major was within a particular college, i.e. The College of Business, the

College of Arts & Architecture, and so on. Each of these colleges had various goals and aligned career paths. I thought that maybe I could do a series of programs: one for each college. I would bring in one or two professionals from related fields and ask them to give some professional tips. I drafted up a flyer and started taking my proposal into meetings with boards, committees, and diversity councils. They were very polite. **Yet there was something in their eyes that told me they were a bit wary of the program.** My gut feeling was confirmed when they'd ask, "So... why is the old program ending again?"

The deans for diversity initiatives did what they could. They sent out the electronic invites to students. I sent out electronic invites to students through our technology system. Then, we all waited.

The program spanned about a week, with four different sessions. Five recruiters/employers came, interested in talking about their company, their company's diversity initiatives, and offering some tips for success. **Ten students came... in total.** Night after night, I sat at my desk with bated breath, hoping that there would be more students next time. After the third one, my ego was really taking a hit. A coworker noticed my silent disappointment and said, "It happens to the best of us".

The program didn't work and I wanted to know why. The good thing was that there wasn't too much money lost; only what we spent in pizza and water. The recruiters offered their services generously since we'd booked them the night before the Career Fair and they would have the opportunity to network.

I talked to my boss, told her the dismal numbers, and waited for the stern disapproval that I knew was coming. However, it never came. She congratulated me for being fiscally responsible in the circumstances and then suggested that I work with the assessment office to create a survey and send it to those who came and those who did not. She suggested focus groups so that we could understand what students wanted and needed most at this point in time. She also suggested that I trust my instincts and try again.

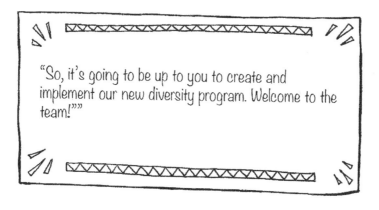

"So, it's going to be up to you to create and implement our new diversity program. Welcome to the team!""

Her belief in me was part of my fuel for success. The surveys told me that the times of the programs were off. I had checked the academic calendar to make sure that I was steering away from exam weeks and other hectic times. However, I did not look at was going on within the institution socially: a rookie mistake that I promised myself I'd never make again. I knew I would do things very differently the next time.

Take two:

Creating things is what I do and I've learned that failure fosters a certain level of creative thinking and troubleshooting. The next semester, I asked a group of students to participate in the planning of the new program. **I reworked the format to be a progressive dinner with a multicultural acting troupe that would act out scenes regarding diversity and the workplace.** Students, recruiters, and employers were all invited. Positive feedback came in after the event and it is something that I'm still very proud of.

It took me multiple tries to get to a comfortable version of success. It took me a lot more time in networking and planning than I'd ever anticipated to get the participant number where we needed it to be. Yet, over time, this story became my favorite fail, because of all I'd learned.

So, what did I learn?

I. Don't take it personally.

This is probably the absolute hardest thing to do. We're invested in our work because our work can speak volumes about who we are. However, it is important to remember that we are not solely defined by the work that we do. When I started talking to colleagues about the programming fail, I learned that I was not the first person to ever have this experience (and I would not be the last). That helped me to redefine my ideas of success to include content first, then student buy-in, and then program participants. For example, the first time around I was solely focused on networking how-to's and resume boosters, which was good content, but it was content that they could get at many of the other workshops across campus. The second time, I changed my content for diverse audiences i.e. discerning a diverse workplace, wearing natural hair to interviews, transitioning during your interview process, being asked illegal questions pertaining to marital status, or navigating the visa questions as an international student. **This shift in the content, made for more student buy-in, which in turn, prompted more people to participate in the program.**

It's very tempting to shirk back and heal your ego by doing some negative navel-gazing. But that's not effective. **Don't write any invitations to your pity party... start strategizing towards your next success.**

II. Strategize Towards Success.

I'm grateful for a supervisor who taught me this skill: **to use the tools at your institution to craft successful initiatives.** At that point, it meant looking at our student affairs research branch to gain answers about why students had not participated and what they were looking for in their next experience. At other institutions, it means including student leaders within the planning process, so that they can organically offer qualitative feedback on everything from the format, to the time, to the marketing materials. It also means asking various stakeholders good questions at the beginning of the process. It means having meetings with faculty members to talk about the work they are doing, their learning outcomes, and how my programming can assist them in creating these outcomes. **This builds rapport, relationships across the institution, and allows for stronger programming experiences.**

III. Look at what large social activities are happening on campus.

If there is one thing I learned, **it is to pay equal attention to the social calendar.** Yes, it may be December, and graduating seniors may or may not know how to maximize their break. Yes, the Career Fair might be coming and exam week might be the week after. **However, do not neglect that students will also invest in their own work/life balance, as well, especially at institutions where over-programming is a salient feature.** Sometimes, they will choose to go to the large philanthropic event or the featured artist concert that coincides with the timing of your program. And that's okay. Just make sure that you go into these scenarios with eyes wide open. Ask your students what else might be going on during the time of your initiatives. You'll be surprised at what you learn! (Disclaimer: you also may have to interject when the details of the social calendar get too "real". Boundaries, boundaries, boundaries!).

IV. Don't duplicate efforts.

This can be quite the challenge if you work or intern at a larger institution. I did not know that students were already making use of similar programming initiatives, within their own college, and tended to be a bit wary of stepping away from those. I only learned this when I started to have lunch and collaborative brainstorming sessions with professionals from other colleges and departments on campus. This allowed me to see if there was something similar that existed already within the institution, because if it did, the chances were that students would gravitate toward it instead.

Failing forward is all about gathering information and managing our emotional responses. No matter how many pretty words we can think to wrap around the concept of failure, it still...well... stinks. **However, it is the way in which we fail that tells our colleagues about our character, our ability to gather information, and our willingness to persist.**

Jade Perry is a student affairs professional that has worked in the areas of multicultural programs, academic advising, and career services! She is an alumni of Penn State University's College Student Affairs program and also holds a B.A. in Integrative Arts from Penn State University. She loves what she does and loves writing about what she does within the field of student affairs! Please feel free to connect with her via Twitter (@SAJadePerry1)!

The Cycle of Avoidance - Renee Dowdy

Sometimes, actually, often times, **we are our greatest enemy to our own success.**

I remember my time as a hall director fondly. I viewed my hall as a microcosm of the university. Every piece of what students encountered touched our work, from financial aid to admissions. I used this philosophy to guide my relationships, my focus on the big picture, and how I chose to maximize my role with 400 students in the middle of downtown Milwaukee. **I looked back with pride for a long time at my work there until I realized there was part of the story I often glazed over.** And within that was a critical lesson.

During the first year in my role, my job was my greatest escape from a suffering marriage. When I came into the position, that relationship was already on life support. And as it turns out, having an office one floor away from your apartment is an excellent place to hide out when you don't want to deal with what's really happening in life. **I thought I was thriving but really I was caught in a cycle of avoidance.**

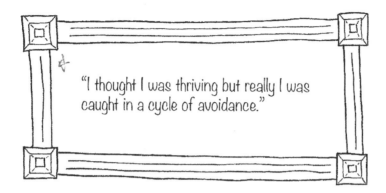

"I thought I was thriving but really I was caught in a cycle of avoidance."

We often wait. We wait for someone else to tell us what to do. We wait for a supervisor to give us guidance. We wait for change. We wait for problems to solve themselves. That's any of us on the days we are likely least proud of. I was using my job, and finding success in it no less, as I waited for a painful and difficult marriage to end. And then one day it did. And I went back to work.

It became my crutch, something reliable, something I could be proud of regardless of what was happening everywhere else. It was constant and rewarding. **But the fact was, I closed myself off from the real hard work of living for the more safe work of doing my job.** It was time to break that cycle.

I began placing workouts on my calendar for the end of the work day. I joined MeetUp groups ranging from brunching ladies to tennis. I traveled. I learned how to cook new things. I let myself open up to the world outside my office and found it paid dividends. I knew what a well and harmonious life could look like but finally did the real work to claim that for myself.

If you are reading this and what you come away with is another message about balance, you're missing the point. **When work is our outlet, we have to question ourselves.** Am I hiding? If so, why? What am I escaping? What is not being fulfilled? When we answer these questions we begin to get closer to our truth versus hiding from the realities of our lives. **Failure is a tricky thing because it can often be first disguised as success.**

There are times when our work requires exceptional time and attention. But these are times the critical step is to distinguish between what is necessary and what we choose. And further, to identify what we choose and why. Yes, sometimes we simply really enjoy our work. Or we start a new job that requires extra time and attention. But I would counter that many times we are in a cycle of avoidance.

I look back on my career and often do not see the failures. I see lessons, times I learned to do things differently. **Failure is most often not seen in the outcome but in the process.** Moreover, our personal failures can teach us just as much about how to navigate our work as our professional experiences. I hope you may have an opportunity to look at your choices and claim what you need in life to experience wholeness at work and at home. And when you trip, because we all do, I hope it will propel you forward. **But that will only happen if you give yourself the time and space to reflect not just on the outcomes, but on the process.**

 Renee Piquette Dowdy is the Assistant Director of Education and Curriculum Design for Synergos, AMC, working primarily with the Association of Fraternity & Sorority Advisors (AFA) and the Association of Fraternal Leadership & Values (AFLV). As a Wisconsinite living in the west, she enjoys hot yoga, hiking, leisurely bike rides, and spending time with her Goldendoodle puppy. Renee enjoys writing and speaking on wellness, organizational culture, and professional development strategies. Connect with her on Twitter: @reneepdowdy.

make the second chance count.

Make the Second Chance Count - Sinclair Ceasar

I will always be thankful for the day I almost lost my job as a recess coach. The afternoon started like any other at the after school program. I ran some high-energy activities, made sure no students died, and fought the urge to look out for the 5 p.m. bell. And then a couple of students decided to break some school policies. They were minor violations, but when I confronted the students about what they did, all I got was "I didn't do anything," and, "Why are you even talking to us?" I was furious. I had no tolerance for disrespect and we were two months from the end of the school year. It had been a LONG year. My patience was thin, and I had to investigate to get to the bottom of a few minor policy violations.

I hadn't been taking care of myself mentally and physically. At this point, I could have had a developmental conversation with the students, decided on what punitive action to take – if any- and let them be on their way. **Instead, I told them each to write, "I will not lie or disrespect others" about 100 times.** I didn't intend to have them actually write the sentence that many times. I was going to stop them when they reached 10 lines of text each, but they never made it that far. One of them decided to contact their parent about the cruel and unusual punishment of the writing assignment. **The parent contacted the after school program and the company I was working for, and mayhem ensued.**

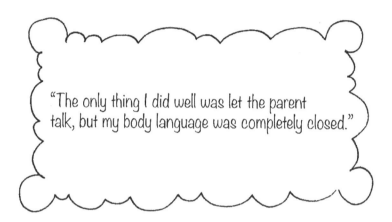

"The only thing I did well was let the parent talk, but my body language was completely closed."

Twenty minutes later, I was sitting in a room with the students in question, the parent who reported me, and staff members from the after school program. The parent wasted no time asking me why I called their child a liar. The room was thick with tension, primarily between the parent and me. **The only thing I did well was let the parent talk, but my body language was completely closed.** At one point I looked down to adjust my watch, and the parent asked me if I had somewhere to be because I appeared to be checking the time. It was an unfavorable situation. When it was my turn to speak, I communicated nothing but a defensive attitude. At some point I confused anxiety with bravado and started to raise my voice a little. Fortunately, one of the after school program staff members stepped in and mediated the situation. All I wanted was to be beamed up to the Starship Enterprise and travel light years away.

Finally the meeting ended. The students were prompted to apologize for their behavior, and I apologized for failing as the world's worst adjudicator. I was left alone in the room dazed, hurt, and upset. Moments later, two administrators from my company appeared at the meeting room door. I thought they were there to hear me vent about how difficult and uncomfortable the situation was. Yes, I did vent for three minutes, and I was almost to the point of tears. **I knew I had messed up, but felt like I hadn't been supported either.** The administrators told me about how I could have handled the situation with more compassion. They also informed me the parent had contacted company headquarters and filed a complaint against me. Then they sat in silence while I took in what they told me. A few awkward days at work later, my direct supervisor sat me down in my office and administered a written warning. If warnings counted as points to a cool prize, I'd have been in good shape. His message was for me to use better judgment when working with students and especially when confronting upset parents.

Another Chance

I wasn't fired or let go from the company and finished the year on a stronger note. Two years later, as a graduate hall director, I was faced with a challenging parent situation at 3 a.m. and incurred everything from undue criticism to profane language. I gently asked the parent to close the door to my office and invited them to sit down. **Then I told them I genuinely cared about what they had to say, but I could hear them more clearly if they**

spoke to me calmly because I was feeling a little attacked. They apologized and continued to tell me about their student's issue. I listened and tried my best to let them know I heard them. We worked towards discovering solutions for their situation. No complaints were made to my supervisor and I wasn't written up. **Failure during my position as a recess coach taught me three invaluable lessons.**

#1 – Save the labels for the holiday gifts.

Refrain from labeling students or anyone for that matter. I messed up when I essentially called the students liars, and I forgot to deal with the actual policy violations. **Focus on what happened and what was observable.** There isn't much we can do about a label, but we can work to help stop or encourage a behavior.

#2 – Feel the burn but don't let it consume you.

If you let fear and anger override your judgment, you won't have to question why you failed. Sure, I felt attacked by the parent in the meeting room, but my passive attitude turned rude behavior unnecessarily escalated the situation. It's okay to stop, take a few breaths, and remember why you are in a confrontation or student conflict in the first place: because it's what you signed up for. **The work you do isn't arbitrary so don't make arbitrary decisions.**

#3 – Sharpen your own saw.

Upon arriving to my new job, I hit the ground running at work and on professional growth. **I told my supervisor about my lack of expertise in handling parent confrontations.** They immediately had my back and gave me feedback whenever I was blindsided by an upset parent. I wanted to be more proactive about sharpening my own saw, so I was hyper-vigilant whenever a parent came into the central office with a complaint. I watched how other administrators managed their emotions, and calmly addressed the parents. **Then, I put what I learned into practice and eventually became a go-to person for certain parent situations.**

I hate failing. Perfectionism runs through my blood, but it's going to happen. I'm going to drop the ball. I'm okay with that. **I'm not okay with failing backwards and repeating my mistakes.** Ever since the day I almost lost my job, I have made every effort to fail forward and fail into better choices, better judgment, and better memories for my students and all others who are impacted by the work I do with any organization.

 Sinclair is currently an Assistant Director of Student Life at Loyola University, and is an editor at the Student Affairs Collective. Inquire about speaking/workshops or just keep the conversation going by contacting him at sceasar1@gmail.com and check out more at www.TheSAProNextDoor.com

ADMIT IT, ACCEPT IT, grow.

Admit It, Accept It, Grow - Emily Holmes

We've really got to become more comfortable as humans as well as student affairs professionals at being honest about our failures. We mold students, for goodness sake! **We have conversations with them about their failures as learning opportunities, why don't we talk as freely about our own?** I say we because I am right there with ya. Do I always show my weakness? No! Do I admit that I messed up? Rarely! Maybe it's because my top strength is Achiever so I, naturally, don't ever want anyone to think I'm not capable of excelling at something (maybe some of this is myself not wanting to accept that I can't do everything 100% all the time either but that's another story). Maybe it is because I am an introvert so I prefer to process feelings and emotions internally versus openly with others. Either way, I'm working to accept my failures- embrace them rather- and give myself some grace in the process.

A couple years ago I switched positions on campus and was thrust into the role of supervising staff. Granted, I read the job description and was familiar with what the job would entail so I knew what I was getting myself into. I exercised some thoughts of doubt and worry that I wouldn't be up to this new task but ultimately knew that this was a necessary next step I needed to take so I accepted the challenge.

Whoa! WHY don't we have more professional development out there for new supervisors? Or just supervisors in general? There was no training that came with this role. This was a totally new job description for me and within just a few weeks, I knew I was in way over my head. Supervising is tough and I was failing. I was finding it hard to communicate with my staff so I just stopped communicating altogether. **I didn't want them to not like me so I was avoiding difficult conversations.** I wasn't listening to what they actually needed from me because I was too busy giving them to-do lists to make sure that things in the office were getting accomplished. **As a result, I suffered and my staff suffered with me.**

"I didn't want them to not like me so I was avoiding difficult conversations."

I reached a point where I was desperately searching for resources. How to set expectations for staff? How to manage first-year professionals? How to handle difficult situations as a leader? Through some independent research, I found ACPA's

Mid-Level Management Institute and applied on a whim. I was accepted into the institute, attended in January of 2014 and thus began a six-month soul-searching professional development process. At MMI, we were challenged to do some "head to heart" thinking: **be vulnerable and open with staff and others so we can learn from one another;** ask staff questions about themselves and show them things previously kept guarded about fears of being a bad or incapable supervisor. My issues really boiled down to my fear of thinking, **"Am I enough?"**

As a woman and as a mother, I think I will always experience a struggle to "do it all" and "keep it all together" since I am always going in so many directions. **But as a professional, there is immense growth and possibilities attached if you can throw aside these fears and really be present and open with your staff.** They will be more receptive to you and your leadership if they can really learn WHO you are- even with admitting the failures.

After MMI, I had some tough (for me) conversations with my staff (ones in which I might have cried). **I put it all out there by first apologizing for not being the best supervisor I could be, not because I was incapable, but because I was just doing it wrong.** I promised to listen better. To ask for their opinions more often. To show more vulnerable parts of myself to them on a regular basis. **They were extremely appreciative of my honesty and I'm happy I took that step.** Some days are still a challenge but I feel I am in a much better place now than I was and am learning and taking more risks every day. The "failing" aspect of putting myself out there doesn't scare the crap out of me now as much as it once did. I share with you some of the key takeaways I'd pass onto folks who feel like they are failing as supervisors:

1. Be clear with your staff about your expectations.

Setting expectations early is crucial. It's true that your staff needs to see you as a leader who models these expectations, too. But you also need to clearly discuss with them these expectations in person. When they are not followed, quick follow-up to address the issue is always key versus letting it go or being passive aggressive about it.

2. Include them in conversations and decision making as much as possible.

Your staff will feel like you care if they feel valued. Bring them with you to meetings so they can learn. Teach them about processes you handle in the office. Ask their opinions on new projects or decisions you have to make it. Actually TAKE their advice or suggestions so you aren't just asking for opinions you'll never put into practice. Explain to them as much as you can about why you are making the decisions you are when you do.

3. Give yourself permission to be honest about not having all the answers.

Sometimes the best thing you can say when someone asks you a question you don't have an answer to is just that. Be honest with yourself that supervising doesn't mean "knows everything". There's great learning potential when you can work together with your staff as a team on a project or in finding a solution to a problem that you couldn't do on your own. Seeing your staff accomplish things like that makes you feel like a good supervisor because it's promoting teamwork and developing new skill sets for everyone.

4. See supervising as less about you and more about them.

Spend time with your staff and get to know them as people, not just professionals. Take an interest in them and ask lots of questions. They will start to feel like you care about them- not just in a "this person can get the job done" way but in the real way. The real potential an area has to shine lies in how well its people get along and how much trust and respect is valued.

A successful supervisor is not a perfect one without failures. **A successful supervisor is one who finds value in the art of continually learning to understand people and ourselves.** Failing makes experiences worthwhile. We come out stronger, smarter and braver. **We can create a better environment for our staff and ultimately touch more students as well.**
When is the last time you failed and lived to learn from it and talk about it? I challenge you to try it and join in the conversation as we all fail forward.

 Emily Holmes is the Associate Director for Programs at The University of Southern Mississippi. There she oversees student involvement including student organization management, event registration and leadership development for over 200 student organizations. Follow her on Twitter @emilydholmes.

STAND UP EIGHT

Stand Up Eight - Kate McGartland

My story is one of failure, perseverance, resilience and growth. It is not a piece of me that I have shared widely before now, but the lessons are more valuable than my apprehension, so here goes...

Between the winter of 2011 and the summer of 2012, I applied for 37 positions, went on nine interviews, and received zero offers. I was working for an institution that was not a good professional fit for me, was living alone in a city that was far from friends, family, and at that point had lived apart from my (now former) spouse for four years. Life was not easy to say the least. I felt stuck in a "no-end-in-sight" cycle of failure – each new appealing job prospect brought a renewed sense of hope that was quickly struck down with a result that had become a little too familiar. If I made it to the interview stage, the feedback was consistent: "You were great," "there's nothing more you could have done," "we would have selected you if we didn't have an internal candidate." While these comments may seem positive, they are not what you want to hear again and again. You start to think "What's wrong with me?" You start to see this as nothing but failure. And failing over and over again, for a long period of time, is not a fun place to be. Combining this with my lack of patience made this job search acutely agonizing.

As disheartened as I was after each rejection, I knew I had to persevere. I gave myself the time to be upset, but then picked myself up, dusted myself off, and kept going. **There is such a fine line separating** *the breaking point* **from** *breaking through* **that when you're ready to give up - and give in to failure - is when you need to push through the most.** I knew that, and refused to let failure get the best of me.

The 38th application I submitted led me to where I was meant to be. I went to work for a department that was innovative, supportive and engaging, and an institution committed to student success and employee growth and development. I worked with colleagues who were dedicated, talented, and student-centered. I saw the impact of my work daily, weekly and annually. It was truly fulfilling work and I was so thankful to have found such a great professional fit. Since then, I have moved into a role that challenges me to look at higher education and the student experience in a much different way, and I feel completely at home. If I hadn't "failed" 37 times before this, I would not be where I am today. **Turns out, failure leads you to exactly where you need to be.**

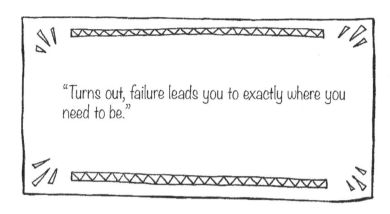

"Turns out, failure leads you to exactly where you need to be."

Yes, it is easy for me to look back now and understand why I needed to go through those 18 months. Retrospect is an incredible teacher. When I was in the middle of my struggle, I did not, and could not, understand why things were happening the way they were. If you are being challenged by failure or struggle, I hope that the lessons I learned from my experience will resonate with you. They have been invaluable learning for me:

1. Build & Rely On Your Support Network.

I believe that relationships are the cornerstone of life. We rarely do anything alone, and having a solid support network is crucial to getting through the tough times.**Have key people within your support network that you trust and respect and do not be afraid to lean on them.** Know who to turn to when you just need to vent, when you need a shoulder to cry on, and when you need a kick in the pants (this may not be the same person).

2. Find Fulfillment.

Put time into building a full life, so that work is not the only thing you have. Volunteer at the humane society, star in a local theatre production, make time for family and friends, take a vacation (or a staycation), or join that running club. **Do things that bring you joy and fulfillment that are not tied to work.** This way, if work is challenging (and not in Sanford's Challenge & Support kind of way), you have a whole host of things to keep you motivated.

3. Be Patient.

Things may not always happen on your timeline. Take time to understand what you want and set goals to help you get there. **Try to be patient with the process and trust that it is unfolding as it should.** (I recognize that this is a lot easier said than done, and it is something that I continue to work on.

4. Push Through.

When you face failure, take the time to process it, but do not reside there. Do what you can to move forward. Reflect on past challenges, and remember how you got through those times. **Use that strength to push through and persevere.**

5. Celebrate.

Failure is not forever. **When you overcome obstacles to achieve your goals, take the time to celebrate.** Reflect on the lessons learned through the process, and then do something special just for you. Don't forget to include those who supported you through the process – they will want to share in your celebration!

To close, I want to share a quote that has become a bit of a mantra for me:

"Fall down seven times, Stand up eight."

–Japanese Proverb

If I ever muster up the strength to get a tattoo, it will be of that quote. It is a constant reminder that there will be setbacks in life, but working through them and coming out stronger is the reward.

Kate currently serves as the Director of Student Support Services within the Online Learning Services division of Pearson North America, where she provides leadership to the Student Services team, analyzes results and strategizes to improve student retention. In her down time, Kate enjoys exploring the city she calls home (Toronto) and is an avid reader and blogger and tries to travel to a new city each year. You can follow Kate on Twitter: @Kate_McGartland

– embrace the errors –

Embrace the Errors - Chris Conzen

Many of us have been in this situation before: you unveil a new program or initiative, it goes well and you're feeling pretty good about introducing something fresh or different. Most people are complimentary and give you a pat on the back...but there's that one person who just can't wait to tell you what you did wrong. **From the moment your idea started, that person was already staring with a magnifying glass ready to catch the minor snag or malfunction, and they are sure to let you know about it.**

When this happens to me, I generally go through the Idina Menzel stages of emotion – there's the anger (no good deed goes unpunished) the defiance (take me or leave me) the acceptance (let it go) and then the recommitment (I'm flying high, defying gravity). If imperfection is a gift, as our Student Affairs sage, Brene Brown, tells us, then I'm like Richie Rich on Christmas morning. **I'm quite comfortable with failing, in part because I practice reflection.** I know my mistakes almost as soon as they have happened, and I'm ready and willing to not just admit them, but to learn from them as well. While at times I might be a tad overly self-critical, I have come to a point of being able to not allow my failures to outweigh my successes in my own mind – and to recognize those times when the failures actually do.

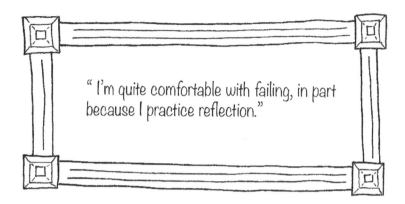

"I'm quite comfortable with failing, in part because I practice reflection."

But my message is not to my brothers and sisters in "flawsomeness". **I'm directing this to those who feel the need to keep what I like to call the failure scorecards.** These are the individuals who keep meticulous notes on where others go wrong; the folks who are, in fact, more comfortable noticing the speck of dust in the eye of another while ignoring the plank in their own.

Some of you might have rationalized this behavior into a form of motivation. By pushing others to always do "better", you convince yourself, you're pushing them to be the best versions of themselves. And this strategy might work on occasion. **But the danger of this behavior is that it can breed mistrust and resentment and actually stifle growth. Innovation requires risk.** Attempting to do something that hasn't been done before means it hasn't been tested. There will inevitably be bugs to work out and adjustments to be made. But if those who work with or for you are convinced that your feedback will always be critical, at some point the intrinsic motivation may no longer be enough. Instead, they will be more inclined to mimic practices they know are likely to receive the least negative feedback.**People will no longer grow, but rather, maintain.** People will tell you and give you what you want to hear instead of what you should hear. In the end, you have strengthened others, but actually weakened yourself.

So you're the scorecard keeper? Congratulations, acceptance is the first step! So what can you do to try to change this behavior?

1. Don't burst the bubble.

It's not likely that you will forget what didn't go right with a program, initiative, or idea, but is it really necessary to share that information immediately? If the initiative was generally a success, allow the individual to bask in that for a moment before deflating the elation.

2. Process instead of prescribe.

When you finally do take the opportunity to offer feedback, process *with* the individual instead of *for* them. Ask them, "how did you think it went overall?" "What do you think went well?" "Is there anything you might do differently or adjust for next time?" If the individual feels supported by you overall, then he or she is more likely to give an honest assessment, and they just might identify what needs improvement on their own.

3. Reframe.

Instead of telling a person what they did wrong, try, instead, to *teach* them how they might improve. Your critical feedback might very well be based on your own rich knowledge and could be quite beneficial. Someone else is more likely to hear and absorb it if it's perceived to come from a place of caring about helping the individual do better rather than making it seem that you want to prove that you ARE better.

4. Don't cross the praise and criticism streams.

Sometimes we think if we lead into critical feedback by cushioning it with praise, it will be taken less harshly. But what ends up happening is that the other individual doesn't even hear the praise because it's immediately washed out by the criticism. Critical feedback IS important to give, but if praise is deserved and warranted, then make sure it is allowed to stand on its own.

We can talk about "failing forward" all we want, but the reality of failure is that it doesn't happen in a vacuum. People can fail forward onto the next step or into a pit. **To create a system that allows failing forward to actually be a progression requires the rest of us imperfect souls to serve as spotters to either nudge back up or, when necessary, catch before they crash.** If we truly value authenticity, then we need to accept that with authenticity comes imperfection.

Persian rugs are said to be created with an intentional imperfection – they are "perfectly imperfect, and precisely imprecise"- and that is how you can determine an authentic

Persian rug from an imposter. When we are able to embrace and appreciate those perfect imperfections in those who work with and for us, we then gain the benefit of their authenticity and all the beauty they have to offer.

 Chris Conzen is a leadership educator with 15 years in student affairs. Chris currently serves as the Assistant Dean of Student Life at LIM College in New York City. Prior to his assignment at LIM College, Chris spent 8 ½ years leading the activities office at a community college.

TRANSPARENCY IN ROUGH TIMES

Transparency in Rough Times - Marci Walton

In light of the new Fail Forward initiative, I had to throw my incredible "fail" into the world. My first year at my current job was a rough one. Rough transition, distinctly unique campus culture, disjointed professional team, and a student staff that I not only inherited, but inherited from the previous Resident Director who more or less walked on water in their eyes. While I spent a good amount of that year **feeling all the feelings,** I came out of it stronger, more confident, and a better leader than before.

I came into that year feeling pretty confident. I had come off four incredible years at a very similar institution, so I felt like my transition wouldn't be too intense. Boy was I wrong! Even though both institutions were in the same state, same size, similar student culture, and were both Catholic and Jesuit, the departmental cultures were wildly different. Additionally, the students I supervised wanted a ton of support, but were confused when I held them accountable. They wanted extensions when they were struggling, but wanted me to be consistent with their peers. **I was being pulled in every direction and never felt grounded in my decision-making.** In addition to this dynamic, my hall is collaboratively run by a Leadership Team consisting of myself, a live-in Faculty Director, Resident Minister, and Assistant

Resident Director. Therefore, most major decisions had to go through a vetting process with this team, something that I now appreciate, but felt stifling at the time.

All of this came to a head when the mother of one of my RA's passed away very suddenly at the beginning of Winter Quarter. I leaped into action, meeting with the RA, offering condolences, asking how I could assist, and working with my supervisor to hold his room and position while he took the quarter off to be with his family. I quickly drafted an email to my entire team, letting them know what was happening and how we were going to support Miguel* by taking all of his RA responsibilities and dividing them amongst team members. I sent flowers to the service and we all created cards to send to his family.

I was shocked when rumblings of unhappiness on the team with how I handled the situation started to emerge. My Assistant RD stated that the team felt like I was cold and uncaring, lacked empathy about the situation, and that I only cared about the work getting done. **In short, I was failing them.** I immediately went on the defensive, called old RAs to get their feedback, processed with my colleagues, all in the hopes of building up a mental wall titled, "See, I'm not the problem, YOU are!" What I failed to do was consider the following:

1. I failed to properly articulate how I was supporting Miguel.

> No one on the team knew about my meetings with Miguel before he left or the phone conversations we had.

I never articulated that I had sent flowers or worked with Housing and Academic Services to hold his space on campus so he could freely leave to be with his family. In the moment, it would have felt like bragging, but looking back, the only thing my team knew was that Miguel's tasks needed to be covered, which came off as cold and not student-centered. In my rush to "handle" things, the human connection that I made with Miguel got lost.

2. I failed to acknowledge the cultural differences that impacted the team dynamic.

Half of my team that year identified as Latino/a and four of them were undocumented students, including the RA who lost his mother. They all had an incredibly tight bond and really felt like family. When we went on a staff retreat to repair relationships, they all mentioned how they wanted to process the loss of Miguel's mother, because to them, she was extended family. This came as a total shock to me, because my upbringing taught me to grieve in private. To pack away your emotions, not to make a scene, and never "burden" someone else with your thoughts. Through my cultural lens, it never occurred to me that my team was not only grieving the loss, but wanted to do so collectively and in community.

3. I failed to access my Leadership Team's support, in fear of looking incompetent.

I rarely shared what was going on to my Leadership Team that year. The structure of collective decision-making was a new one, and I wanted to appear confident, competent, and like I had it all together. By failing to key them into strife until much later on, they weren't able to support me or help me problem-solve the issues at hand.

4. I failed to see/admit to the warning signs earlier in the year.

Hindsight is 20/20 and looking back now, I can see pockets of tension or unresolved issues on the team, going all the way back to summer training. It shouldn't have come as a surprise when the team imploded, but I had on positivity blinders. I easily passed off awkward moments, sideway glances, inside jokes, and seating configurations of staff meetings as a one-time issue, instead of seeing them as symptoms of a sick team.

While the team never felt like a tight unit, we were able to finish out the year. We went on a much-needed retreat, set new expectations, had individual meetings to air our grievances, allowed for personal, quiet reflection time, and I owned up to how I had failed them as a supervisor.

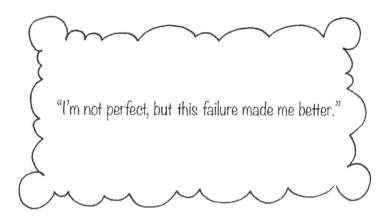

"I'm not perfect, but this failure made me better."

As a result of this team, I supervise differently. I ask the team to communicate with each other when they need a deadline extended. I ask my student leaders very direct questions about expectations they have of me and of one another. **I no longer assume anything. I stick up for myself. I rely on my Leadership Team.** I facilitate more dialogues about personal stories and backgrounds to help ground relationships throughout the year. I am much more aware of awkwardness during the formational times of the group and do my best to address it immediately. I continue to work on being transparent with decision-making. **I'm not perfect, but this failure made me better.**

 Marci Walton is proud to serve as the Assistant Director for Academic Support and Learning Communities for Residence Life at Loyola University Chicago. She is interested in residence life, social justice, service, and the intersections of identity. She is passionately curious about social media, women's leadership, and finding the perfect spot to admire Lake Michigan. Marci can be found on Twitter @MarciKWalton and blogs regularly at www.marcikwalton.com.

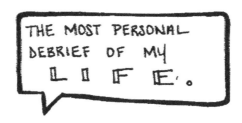

The Most Personal Debrief of my Life - Jared Ward

I am incredibly passionate about working in the cross-section of student affairs and social entrepreneurship. Over the course of my three years at UMass Boston (I was a transfer student), I founded and cultivated a chapter of the global nonprofit organization Enactus.

Enactus is a nonprofit centered in **empowering communities through sustainable social entrepreneurship projects.** Enactus organizations function on college campuses nationally and globally.

In addition to social entrepreneurship I am passionate about **hands-on learning**. After four incredibly triumphant (and chaotic) semesters with Enactus, I allowed less experienced members to begin to step up and take the reigns in our fifth semester in preparation for my impending graduation.

However, **I allowed our rapid past successes to overshadow my better judgment.** Goals went unmet, projects fell apart, and deadlines came and went with no measurable progress. **I was**

pushing members to be independent, but not providing adequate support.

When it came time for the annual conference for Enactus teams around the nation to present on their work, we fell flat on our face. **It felt like my heart was being torn out.** We had literally put blood, sweat, and tears into our work. But, we "failed" to meet the necessary checkpoints for our projects.

I knew my team felt even worse than I did. There were tears, and immediate looks of disbelief. We sat in a conference hall filled with 2,000+ attendees as the news was delivered that we had not succeeded in our goal to reclaim our title as a top 40 ranked organization in the network.
I knew that my teammates would be looking at me to mirror my behavior. **Full disclosure, I am an extrovert and I wear my emotions on my sleeve.** I had to strategically figure out how to use every aspect of this experience as a learning opportunity. I succeeded in doing so and conducted **the most personal and emotionally impacting debrief of my life.**

As changemakers, we are constantly pushing ourselves to succeed. Why would we strive for anything else? But to some, it does not matter how we get there, what we learn in the process, or what we are forced overcome; we just need to meet an end goal. After all, we are socially programmed to have adverse feelings towards mistakes, and towards failures. The very words themselves are respectively defined as "not correct" and "lacking success".

However, is something that is not correct always wrong? **If we lack success on our first try, is that to mean that success is no longer attainable?**

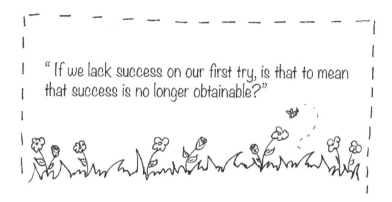

"If we lack success on our first try, is that to mean that success is no longer obtainable?"

We often tell ourselves "I've got this!" or cheer others on "you're going to be great!" **Only to awkwardly later skirt through the conversation in which you must offer advice and condolence when a mark is missed or a goal is not achieved.**

What if we are not missing a mark, but rather just on a trajectory towards an unforeseen destination? What if we are just throwing spaghetti at the wall and seeing what sticks?
With Enactus, I realized that **while we missed our original goal, we succeeded in creating projects to empower underserved communities.** While our new members struggled to stay afloat in more cumbersome roles, we were also preparing organizational leaders for coming years. As a team, we identified where we needed to be stronger, and made the necessary improvements to prepare for the future. **The award did not matter any more, the experience was what mattered.**

Personally, I am a realist. I refuse to sugarcoat situations and I focus on the facts. It is not because I am vindictive or hard pressed to provide sympathy. **It is because I believe that I grew up in a generation that was coddled into wasting time with white lies and attempts at saving face, rather than practicing some honest constructive criticism.**

I am a Millennial, part of the generation that was given trophies for participation, and awarded for coming in last place. Some argue that this cheapens our understanding of failures, but I disagree. I think if anything, our failures are made more salient than ever before. We are given consolation prizes and smaller trophies, tangible representations to show that we are less than others.

I believe that in life there are no mistakes, rather opportunities for growth and development. Nelson Mandela once said, "Our greatest glory in living lies not in never falling, but rising every time we fall". We fall so we can get up. Get up and learn, get up and grow, get up and recover with a fire in our bellies to be better than our last attempt.

With Enactus, we dissected each part of our year and learned from areas that we strayed from our path of success. We walked away with a smaller trophy as a reminder that we must work harder. **This was a humility check, like most failures, that provided a substantial learning opportunity.**

Yes, I like facts and the fact of the matter is we all fail. Not only do we fail, but we will all be told at least once that our ideas are outlandish, or illogical. I challenge you to take naysayers beliefs and use that to fuel you. **Go big or go home. FAIL.** Because it is not how many failures we encounter on our journey, but rather what we choose to do with our failures that defines our success.

Jared T. Ward received his M.Ed from the University of Georgia. He has a vested interest in exploring the cross-section of higher education and social change; and how we can utilize co-curricular learning programs as a means for leadership development through dynamic, equitable, and outcomes focused educational experiences. He holds positions with Lion Leadership, Leadershape, and his alma mater. You can learn more about him at jaredtward.com.

paralyzed by failure

Paralyzed by Failure - Tim St. John

Just a few months ago, something happened to me. Looking back it seems so trivial and silly, but at the time it wasn't. The sweating, the not being able to sleep, the mental roller coaster – it was all very real, however seemingly unnecessary.

The situation was this: it was late at night and we were using technology for our online ticket sales for senior week for the first time. Here was a chance for me to show my ability to innovate to make positive change in my new role. The system crashed. My inbox was immediately flooded with angry and confused emails. I took them personally, too personally. Here I was at 11 p.m. on a Monday sitting at my kitchen table feverishly typing away. No sooner did I decide to email the class and tell them we would try again tomorrow, the server that had crashed switched back on and tickets were sold out. To say students were upset would be an understatement.

I was physically ill. I had just been in my new position as director for four months. This was my first interaction with many of these students and their last experience at our institution. I didn't sleep at all that night. I was unnerved by the fact that there was nothing I could do to fix this and come up with a solution RIGHT

NOW. I wanted a quick fix and I was not going to rest until this had been resolved.

Racing through my head were all sorts of overly dramatic and unrealistic scenarios of students taking over my office space or emailing the President's office. **I was fearing the worst and that worst was what was keeping me up and making me sick.**

Long story short, I did what I do best – I adapted and came up with a creative solution grounded in making sure our students had a positive experience. The next day, I went into fixer mode, doing what I do best by working under pressure. The solution worked and my inbox was again flooded with emails of appreciation. Here's the thing – the solution was not rocket science. In fact, I had solved much bigger problems, even a crisis before including an artist not showing up to our major event just weeks before. As a professional, I pride myself most on my ability to innovatively problem solve. **Why is it that I could not remind myself of that enough to alleviate much of my worry on this particular occasion?**

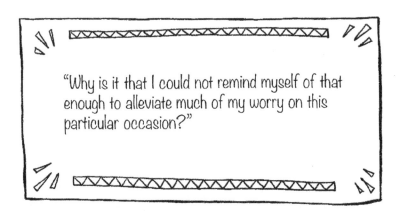

"Why is it that I could not remind myself of that enough to alleviate much of my worry on this particular occasion?"

After much reflection, I can't figure out why this was different. I have never been this affected by something so small, let alone at work. I am always the strong one, with positivity as his top strength, who others look to in situations like this. Perhaps it was the pressure of a new job, baby on the way, and building a home that added up and decided to rear its head that night. Perhaps I was worried that this would significantly impact how others viewed me at my new institution. Others' perceptions of me have always been something that matter to me, but it had never affected me like this. Perhaps it was something more serious. Whatever happened, this situation has taught me a lot about myself and how to ease my anxiety when future situations like this arise, because they surely will. Here are a few of the lessons I learned that will hopefully help you if you are ever paralyzed by failure:

1. I am, without a shadow of a doubt, my own worst critic.

If this is true for you, you need to own it. Know when you are worried about something or when you make a mistake, that others may not take it to be as bad as you do. Do not let that inner critic be the strongest voice. Find others who help build you up when something goes wrong. My supervisor was that person for me in this situation.

2. Our failures do not define us.

Mistakes happen. The sum of your work is always greater than one mistake. One mistake or failure will not define you. In the story of your life, a failure might be a chapter, a page, or even a sentence. It will never be the whole story. Remembering this gives me solace.

3. Everyone makes mistakes.

This is so simple, yet so important. Not that it makes it any easier, but no one you work with is perfect. You won't be the only one who fails. This is also very important to remember as a colleague or supervisor when others fail. We all need to be patient and flexible with each other.

4. How you respond after failure is key.

How you fix or solve the problem is how you will be remembered. Let the same energy that caused you to get so worried and upset about what would happen fuel your desire to solve the problem. Reflecting and learning from that failure is also essential.

5. Not everything can be fixed immediately.

Sometimes there is truth and power in the statement "There is nothing I can do right now." If I would have remembered that, I would have slept that night. We live in an immediate society where everything needed to be done yesterday. Oftentimes, the most important decisions take time. Don't rush foolishly into reacting to a failure.

6. It's ok to get upset when you fail.

I am thankful for this experience. It was the first time since I was a new professional that something work related caused me to get this upset. I was more upset with my failure to appropriately deal with my failure than I was the failure itself. In fact, the problem was out of my hands entirely. Be easy on yourself. Some situations will cause you to get upset. Getting further upset by your response will just make it worse and inhibit your ability to learn and problem solve.

7. Own what you can, release what you can't.

I did not cause the server to crash. I sent the email that told students we would revisit the next day. I did not know the server was back on as that email was sent causing tickets to be sold out. The situation was not my fault, but it was my problem. There is a big difference there. It is easier to solve a problem than it is to address failure. Learn to look at your failures as problems that can be solved. The reframing of that has helped me in recent situations where mistakes can be fixed. When failure happens and there is nothing that can be fixed you need to own it, learn from it, apologize if necessary, and make sure it does not happen again.

Tim currently serves as Director of Student Leadership and Programming at Clark University in Worcester, MA. He is an involved professional currently serving as the Web and Social Media Coordinator for the Association of College Unions-International Region VIII. Connect with Tim on Twitter @timstjohn.

Balancing Fearing Failure & Failing Fearlessly - Joe Ginese

I blame Thomas Edison for the perplexing issue of discussing failure within professional circles. It was Edison who, while describing the trials and tribulations of inventing the lightbulb, that said, "I didn't fail 10,000 times, I learned 10,000 ways how not to make a light bulb." **Well played Edison but time to face the facts, you failed.**

In today's professional society there are two parties at play, **one that fails fearlessly failing and one that fears failure.** It isn't a strict dichotomy; there are those who prefer to dance in the middle.

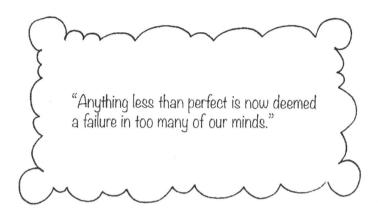

"Anything less than perfect is now deemed a failure in too many of our minds."

Failing fearlessly is becoming a badge of honor in this growing nation of entrepreneurship. Books, articles, and blogs highlight failing fast, failing forward, failing fantastically as badges of honor. In higher education particularly, we are attaching ourselves to these buzz phrases along with buzzwords such as rebels, innovators, and dare I say, instigators. **We don't say we failed, we quickly think of Edison and say we had a learning moment.**

Fearing failure as part of this growing nation of public reputations helps everyone put up the highlight reel of successes. I'm not going to show any failure so let me only mention or share my successes. Let me not draw outside the lines because I don't want to try something new...I might fail. **Anything less than perfect is now deemed a failure in too many of our minds.**

Now, I fear failure just as much as maybe you do, but I also fail fearlessly which maybe you don't. I'm somewhat fearless when it comes to asking big questions, proposing new ideas, or holding people accountable. I'm also somewhat fearful that when I try a new idea that it is going to fail to meet my (and the public's) expectations. "The fear makes me work smart. The fearlessness makes me work hard."

Failure is not bad. Failure is not good. Failure is going to happen. Edison was correct, he did indeed learn from his own and his team's failures. That was his choice. **The issue I have is that people are too comfortable failing under the guise of "Well, I didn't fail, I just learned how NOT to do it."** This does not work. If your enrollment manager doesn't meet the goal of enrolled number of students they wouldn't say, "Oh I didn't fail to meet the admissions goals, I learned what strategies won't work." If they did, chances are they have a fresh resume for you to review.

Here are my suggestions for balancing the fear of failure and failing fearlessly:

– Own failure.

> If you failed, stop trying to mask it or rephrase it. Own your failure and get comfortable with it so you can recognize when it happens. Will this be difficult? Absolutely, but if you try to hide it or choose not to recognize it you will never improve and start thinking that you are flawless (you aren't).

– Share failure.

> I'm not saying you have to tweet a failure every day or write a blog post about it once a month. Call on your

board of directors and confidence architects and share with them. Let them rebuild your confidence and help you reframe your mindset. These are the folks that will help you understand why the failure happened and how to make sure you don't make the same mistakes again.

– Realize that not everything is saved by calling it a learning experiment.

We are educators and as such, we are experimenters on how to best teach, lead, mentor, train, influence, and build the learners around us. Experiments fail. That's the nature of an experiment. You can't justify a failed class, failed program, or failed campaign with the excuse "well at least we learned what not to do."

– Manage your failures.

Decide which ones make good bits of wisdom to pass on to others either in private conversation or publicly. Have a support system to help you do this. Failure is something we don't want to share openly because we are too often ashamed or embarrassed to admit it.

Failing fearlessly means not that you are going to be cavalier with your efforts and openly try something that is likely to fail. **Failing fearlessly means you know you are taking a (calculated) risk in trying something different but you are prepared to handle any result or outcome.**

Fearing failure puts you at risk for becoming complacent. Complacency breeds mediocrity. **Mediocrity is contagious. Don't be patient zero.**

As an MBA trained, entrepreneurial minded, and education focused professional, Joe has taken his curiosity to task in efforts to advocate for the reinvention of learning experiences and innovation within education. He is currently the New and First Year Student Experience Specialist at Borough of Manhattan Community College. Some call Joe an instigator while others describe him as an innovator. He considers himself a champion for change. Follow him on Twitter @JoeGinese

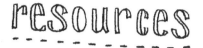

resources

Resources

You Can't Build Cultural Competency Overnight

https://twitter.com/gwendungy
http://www.stirfryseminars.com/pdfs/2014_newsletters/newsletter_march2014.pdf

Failure as a Mentor >
https://www.youtube.com/watch?v=TNXr5Alytg4&feature=kp

Don't Let Fear Be the Driver > http://goo.gl/e6kN8V

Balancing Fearing Failure & Failing Fearlessly > http://ctt.ec/f3ygi

Here's To Your
Continued Success!

a Student Affairs Collective book

Made in the USA
Las Vegas, NV
19 May 2022